Grammar Sense 2A

WORKBOOK

Angela Blackwell

OXFORD
UNIVERSITY PRESS

OXFORD
UNIVERSITY PRESS

198 Madison Avenue
New York, NY 10016 USA

Great Clarendon Street
Oxford OX2 6DP England

Oxford University Press is a department of the University of Oxford. It furthers the University's
objective of excellence in research, scholarship, and education by publishing worldwide in

Oxford   New York

Auckland   Cape Town   Dar es Salaam   Hong Kong   Karachi
Kuala Lumpur   Madrid   Melbourne   Mexico City   Nairobi
New Delhi   Shanghai   Taipei   Toronto

With offices in

Argentina   Austria   Brazil   Chile   Czech Republic   France   Greece
Guatemala   Hungary   Italy   Japan   Poland   Portugal   Singapore
South Korea   Switzerland   Thailand   Turkey   Ukraine   Vietnam

OXFORD and OXFORD ENGLISH are registered trademarks of Oxford University Press.

ISBN: 978 0 19 436622 9

Editorial Manager: Janet Aitchison
Editorial Development, Project Management,
   and Production: Marblehead House, Inc.
Production Manager: Shanta Persaud
Production Controller: Zainaltu Jawat Ali

Illustrations: Roger Penwill, Seitu Hayden
Cover Design: Lee Ann Dollison
Cover Photo: Kevin Schafer / Peter Arnold, Inc.

The authors and publisher are grateful for permission to reprint the following photographs:

p. 1, ©PhotoDisc; **p. 19**: ©Retna Ltd. USA.

The authors and publisher are grateful for permission to reprint the following text excerpts:

p. 12: from "Leaving on a Jet Plane," © Cherry Lane Music. Reprinted with permission; **p. 17:** from
A-Z Encyclopedia of Jokes, © Parade Publications; **p. 19:** from "Robin Williams: Finding His Way
Back," © Readers Digest (UK Edition), March, 1999; **p. 30:** from "Some Will Go the Extra Mile," ©
Copy Right Clearance Center Inc. Reprinted with permission; **p. 60:** from "Weird and Wonderful
Hobbies," © Waldman Publishing. Reprinted with permission.

Every effort has been made to trace and secure permission for all copyright material. In the event of
any oversight or omission, we would appreciate any information that would enable us to do so.

Printing (last digit): 10 9 8 7 6

Printed in Hong Kong

Special thanks to the following students for permission to print their work:
Patty Chow, Mandy Huang, Ryan Chiu

Contents

1 The Simple Present

FORM

Read this letter and complete the tasks below.

Dear Emily
By Emily Fields

Dear Emily,

My husband and I <u>are</u> very happy. He helps me with the housework, doesn't complain, and 5 always remembers my birthday. He is kind and honest. My husband loves me, and I love him.

But I have a problem: My husband doesn't talk to me very

10 much. He goes to work, and when he comes home in the evening, he watches TV. Sometimes he talks to me during the programs, but usually he just sits in silence. I 15 don't know why. He isn't angry at me. He just doesn't seem interested in talking.

I don't go out to work, so I don't have many friends and 20 sometimes I need to talk. But my husband doesn't understand this. What advice do you have?

—Bored in Birmingham

1. There are many verbs in the letter. The first one is underlined. Underline six more.

2. What tense does the writer use in the letter? _____

2) Working on Affirmative and Negative Statements

Complete this text with the simple present form of the verbs in parentheses.

Does your family eat dinner together? Many families don't. A group of high school students was interviewed about what happens at dinnertime in their homes. Here are the results:

Only about half of the students __eat__ (eat) dinner with other family
                                      1

members. These teenagers _____ (enjoy) dinnertime and _____
                              2   3

(see) it as a time to relax and talk.

One boy _____ (talk) to his mother while he is eating, but they often
            4

_____ (argue). And some families _____ (not talk) much
     5   6

during dinner. They _____ (watch) television while they are eating.
                          7

One girl _____ (fix) her own dinner and _____ (eat) it
              8   9

alone. This is often because her parents _____ (not get) home in time to
                                              10

eat dinner with her.

3) Rewriting Affirmative and Negative Statements

Read what Lee says about her English skills and complete the task below.

```
    I don't speak English at home because my parents speak
only Chinese. But I speak English at work and with some
friends. Sometimes my friends correct my pronunciation. I
don't mind that; I think it helps me.
    My listening skills are pretty good. I listen to songs
in English. I watch movies in English, too. My brother
watches them with me.
    Reading and writing are more difficult for me. I don't
read English very often, and I almost never write it. I
think my writing has a lot of grammar mistakes, but maybe I
worry too much.
```

Rewrite Lee's text in the third person (*she*). Change pronouns and the form of the verbs. Do not change anything else.

Lee doesn't speak English at home because her parents speak only

Chinese. But she . . . .

_____

_____

_____

_____

A. Complete these questions with *Do, Does, Is,* or *Are.*

1. <u>Do</u> you like the musicians?

2. _____ you from around here?

3. _____ you like this club?

4. _____ you here with friends, or are you alone?

5. _____ your friend have blond hair and glasses?

6. _____ that her over there?

7. _____ she Armenian, too?

8. _____ she speak English?

B. Match the questions in part A with these answers.

<u>4</u> **a.** I'm with a friend.

_____ **b.** No, she isn't. She's Russian.

_____ **c.** No. I'm from Armenia.

_____ **d.** No, she doesn't. She has dark hair.

_____ **e.** Yes, it is.

_____ **f.** Just a little.

_____ **g.** Yeah. They're OK.

_____ **h.** Yes. It's great.

Read these facts about the United States and complete the task below.

U.S. FACTS
1. Most Americans live near cities.
2. Most people go to work by car.
3. Very few people (five percent) use public transportation to go to work.
4. Most people retire at age 65.
5. Most families have two or more televisions.
6. Many people study at a college or university after high school.
7. Most Americans move every five years.
8. Most American women marry at age 25.

Write information questions for the answers.

1. Where _do most Americans live?_____

   Near cities.

2. How _____

   By car.

3. How many _____

   Very few people. Only five percent.

4. When _____

   At age 65.

5. How many _____

   Two or more.

6. What _____

   They study at a college or university.

7. How often _____

   Every five years.

8. When _____

   At age 25.

MEANING AND USE

6 Understanding the Simple Present

A. Read the paragraphs below. Where does each one come from? Write the letter of the appropriate source next to each paragraph.

SOURCES	
a. advertisement	**d.** biology textbook
b. computer manual	**e.** article from a magazine for parents
c. personal letter	**f.** magazine interview with an athlete

_d_ **1.** All South American monkeys live in trees, and they eat mostly leaves, fruit, and insects. Some African and Asian monkeys spend most of their lives on the ground and eat many different kinds of foods.

_____ **2.** During the baseball season, I always do things a certain way. If I eat some chicken before a game and we win the game, then I eat chicken before every game. After the games, I eat brownies with ice cream.

_____ **3.** Our fruitcake is a great holiday gift for family or friends. It tastes delicious. Everyone loves it. And it costs only $6.99!

_____ **4.** Let's start with some important terms. The *desktop* is what you see on the screen (if you don't have programs on the screen). The desktop has icons. *Icons* are small pictures on your desktop. They represent programs.

_____ **5.** This semester, I have four classes in a row on Mondays, Wednesdays, and Fridays (including one at 8:00 A.M. YUCK!), but Tuesdays and Thursdays I sleep late. I work in the restaurant two nights a week.

_____ **6.** In many families, children help with chores like making beds and doing dishes. Chores teach kids about responsibility and the importance of work. Kids complain about their chores, but they feel better when they do them. Chores make kids an active part of the family.

B. Look back at the paragraphs in part A. Which paragraph uses the simple present to:

_6_ **a.** talk about general truths?

_____ **b.** tell about scientific facts?

_____ **c.** tell about scheduled events?

_____ **d.** describe a person's habits and routines?

_____ **e.** give definitions?

_____ **f.** talk about states (likes, taste, etc.), not actions?

COMBINING FORM, MEANING, AND USE

7) Editing

There are eight errors in this student's composition. The first one has been corrected. Find and correct seven more.

> has
> My country ~~have~~ a tropical climate. The two seasons is summer and winter. Summer go from April to October. In summer it gets very hot. The temperature sometimes reach 40° Celsius. It also rain a lot in summer. Winter in my country begin in November. In winter, it is cooler, and it not rain very much. I like the weather better in the winter because I no like hot weather.

8) Writing

Follow the steps below to write a descriptive paragraph.

1. Think about your routines for Saturday (or for another day of the week). Write a list of the things you usually do on that day.

   Here's an example:

   On Saturday I usually . . .
   - get up at 9:00 A.M.
   - do things around the house
   - work in the garden
   - work on my car
   - repair things
   - have dinner with friends

2. On a separate sheet of paper, write a paragraph describing your routines for the day you chose. Use your notes, and put your activities in the correct time order. Use the simple present.

> On Saturday I usually get up at 9:00 A.M. Then I do things around the house. In the morning, I work in the garden. I rake the leaves and mow the lawn. In the afternoon, I work on my car or repair things. . . .

2 Imperatives

FORM

1 Examining Form

Read this brochure from a car rental company and complete the tasks below.

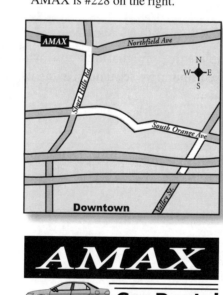

To get to AMAX Car Rental from downtown:
- <u>Drive</u> north on Valley Street.
- Go through two traffic lights.
5 - Turn left onto South Orange Avenue at the third traffic light.
- Stay on South Orange for four miles.
- Make a right onto Short Hills Road.
- Drive for two miles.
10 - Turn left onto Northfield Avenue. AMAX is #228 on the right.

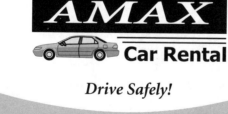

Drive Safely!

15 For further help, please call 1-800-555-AMAX

1. There are nine examples of imperatives in the brochure. The first one is underlined. Underline eight more.

2. Does an imperative sentence have a subject? _____

2 Writing Affirmative and Negative Imperatives

Rewrite these sentences as commands. Use imperatives. You do not have to use all the words.

1. You should turn on the engine.

   Turn on the engine.

2. You need to let go of the hand brake.

   _____

3. You should put the car into drive.

   _____

4. You should check the rearview mirror.

   _____

5. You need to turn the steering wheel to the right.

   _____

6. You shouldn't go so fast.

   _____

3 Working on Affirmative and Negative Imperatives

Use the verbs below to complete the information about what to do in an earthquake. Write affirmative or negative imperative sentences, using capital letters where necessary.

check	know	have

Before an earthquake, _check_ your house for items that may fall down.
                          1

Always _____ a week's supply of food and water in the house.
              2

_____ where to meet your family if an emergency happens.
      3

go	panic	go

During a quake, _____ . If you are indoors, _____ outdoors:
                    4   5

It is more dangerous outdoors. If you are outdoors, _____ to an open area.
                                                          6

move	check	use

After a quake, when the shaking stops, _____ for injuries. If a person has
                                            7

serious injuries, _____ that person; instead, wait for help. If everyone is OK
                      8

and you leave the building, _____ the elevator to leave. Stairs are safer.
                                9

MEANING AND USE

Matching Imperatives

Match the signs to the places.

_e_ **1.** Please wait for the next available
teller.

_____ **2.** Exit here in an emergency.

_____ **3.** In case of fire, use stairs for
exit. Do not use elevator.

_____ **4.** Keep all medicines out of the reach
of children.

_____ **5.** Open this end.

_____ **6.** Please wait to be seated.

_____ **7.** Do not feed the animals.

_____ **8.** Do not disturb.

a. On a door that leads outside a
building

b. In a restaurant

c. On a bottle of aspirin

d. On a box

e. In a bank

f. In a zoo

g. On the door of a hotel room

h. Next to an elevator

5 **Giving Advice**

Complete these tips for air travelers. Use the imperative form of one of the
verbs below.

arrive	bring	call	check	chew	drink	enjoy	fasten	listen	remove

1. _Call_____ the airline a day in advance to confirm your flight.

2. _____ the departure time before leaving home.

3. _____ at the airport at least two hours before your flight.

4. _____ your ticket and at least one form of identification.

5. _____ sharp objects from your hand luggage.

6. On the plane, _____ to the safety announcements.

7. _____ your seat belt.

8. In flight, _____ a lot of water.

9. _____ gum during take-off or landing.

10. _____ your flight!

Match the sentences in the box to the pictures below. Then look again at each picture and circle the correct use of each imperative.

Get up!	Have a seat.	Let me see, please.
Look out!	Don't worry about it.	Hurry up!

1. <u>Hurry up!</u>

   request   directions   (command)

4. _____

   directions   warning   offer

2. _____

   offer   warning   request

5. _____

   offer   command   directions

3. _____

   advice   offer   request

6. _____

   offer   warning   request

COMBINING FORM, MEANING, AND USE

7 **Giving Directions**

Write directions from your house to each of the places below. Use the affirmative and negative imperatives and the expressions in the box when possible.

| turn right | turn left | go to the corner | don't go past | follow |

1. your school

Walk one block and turn right at May Street.

2. your friend's house

_____

3. the post office

_____

4. the bus stop

_____

8 **Writing**

On a separate sheet of paper, write a paragraph in which you give advice to a friend. He or she is moving from a small town to a large city to study. Give your friend advice on some or all of the topics below. Use affirmative and negative imperatives.

using public transportation	meeting new people
walking on the street at night	finding a place to live
keeping valuables (money, credit cards, jewelry, etc.) safe	finding a part-time job
	buying groceries

When you move to _____, don't walk alone on the street late at night. Don't carry a lot of money or wear a lot of jewelry. . . .

3 The Present Continuous

FORM

1 Examining Form

"Leaving on a Jet Plane" is a classic song from the 1970s. Read this excerpt from the song and complete the tasks below.

Leaving on a Jet Plane

All my bags are packed, and I'm ready to go
I'm standing here outside your door
I hate to wake you up to say goodbye
5 But the dawn is breaking, it's early morn
The taxi's waiting, he's blowing his horn
Already I'm so lonesome I could die
So kiss me and smile for me
Tell me that you'll wait for me
10 Hold me like you'll never let me go
'Cause I'm leaving on a jet plane
Don't know when I'll be back again
Oh babe, I hate to go

1. There are five examples of the present continuous in the song. The first one is underlined. Underline four more.

2. How is the present continuous formed? _____

Complete the paragraph with the present continuous form of the verbs in parentheses. Use contractions when possible.

Right now, I <u>'m standing</u> in the living room, and I
_____ (look) out the window. It is a beautiful day, and the sun
_____ (shine). My three boys are in the front yard. They
_____ (play) with a garden hose. They _____
(wear) their new clothes, but they _____ (not/think) about that.
They _____ (have) a wonderful time. My oldest boy
_____ (spray) the two younger ones with the hose. They
_____ (not/run) away. They _____ (try) to get
the hose away from him, and he _____ (not/let) them get the hose.
My wife _____ (tell) him to stop, but he _____
(not/pay) attention. The two younger boys _____ (laugh). They
_____ (get) very wet!

Writing Information Questions

Write information questions about the underlined words and phrases below.

1. You're going <u>somewhere</u>.

   <u>Where are you going?</u>

2. Your friends are traveling <u>somehow</u>.

   _____

3. The boss is talking to <u>someone</u>.

   _____

4. That child is crying <u>for some reason</u>.

   _____

5. Susan and John are going <u>somewhere</u>.

   _____

6. <u>Someone</u> is following us.

   _____

MEANING AND USE

4 **Contrasting Routines with Activities in Progress**

Complete these sentences with *it rains* or *it's raining*.

1. <u>It rains</u> _____ here every night.

2. Oh, no! _____.

3. _____ a lot in January, but it doesn't snow.

4. I don't want to go out because _____.

5. The weather is terrible in November. _____, and it's
   very windy.

6. Let's wait here a while longer. I think _____.

7. _____ every winter for two months, but it's never
   very cold.

8. _____ outside. Don't forget your umbrella.

Read this e-mail and complete the tasks below.

To: Lisa Miller
From: Jada Hal
Cc: Gina Flynn
Subject: Hello from school

Hi, guys!

I'm writing this on Chris's computer. He's studying in the library at the moment. Everything is fine. I'm taking three science classes this semester.

I don't have an apartment right now. For now I'm staying with Maria. Luisa and I are trying to get an apartment together. But the apartments seem very expensive. And rents are going up all the time.

Good-bye for now. My favorite TV show is starting. I'll call you this weekend.

Love,
Jada

Find sentences in the e-mail that are examples of the following uses. Write each sentence under the appropriate use.

1. The present continuous for an activity that is in progress at the exact moment the speaker is talking:

   a. _I'm writing this on Chris's computer._

   b. _____

   c. _____

2. The present continuous for an activity that is in progress but not happening at the exact moment the speaker is talking:

   a. _____

   b. _____

   c. _____

3. The present continuous for situations that are changing:

   _____

4. Stative verbs that are usually used in the simple present:

   a. _____

   b. _____

COMBINING FORM, MEANING, AND USE

Thinking About Meaning and Use

Complete these sentences. Write the simple present or the present continuous forms of the verbs in parentheses. Use contractions when possible.

1. Sasha _is driving_____ (drive) the car, but he _doesn't own___ (not own) it.

2. They _____ (talk) to the teacher because they _____
   (not/understand) the homework.

3. They _____ (build) a new library because the old library _____
   (not/have) enough room.

4. Hector _____ (not/seem) very happy these days. Maybe he
   _____ (work) too hard.

5. He _____ (think) the chapter is easy, so he _____ (not study)
   for the grammar test.

6. _____ you _____ (know) Yoko? She _____ (act) in
   the new play.

7 **Writing**

Follow the steps below to write a descriptive paragraph. Write as much detail as you can. Use the present continuous when possible.

1. Look out a window that has a view of a street.

2. On a separate sheet of paper, write a paragraph describing what is happening. You may want to use some words from the box.

SUBJECTS	VERBS
some people a dog/cat/bird a group of students/children a truck/car	carrying holding moving (toward/away from . . .) reading laughing running standing (near/beside/at . . .)

> It's raining, so there aren't many people outside. Two
> students are running toward the building. Maybe they're
> late for class . . . .

Chapters 1–3

A. Use each set of words to write the question for these question/answer jokes.

1. A: _____? (fish/go/heaven/to/what)

   B: Angel fish!

2. A: _____? (do/face/flowers/have/on/you/your/what)

   B: Tulips (two lips)!

3. A: _____? (old/an/die/does/clock/when)

   B: When its time is up!

4. A: _____? (words/have/the/letters/most/what)

   B: The words *post office*!

5. A: _____? (a/a/does/giraffe/have/long/neck/why)

   B: Because its feet smell bad!

6. A: _____? (a/does/doctor/get/angry/when)

   B: When he has no more patience (patients)!

B. Read these sentences about Saturday afternoon at Alex's house. Find and correct the errors.

7. Today is Saturday, and Alex is stay at home with his family.

8. His mother makes a chocolate cake in the kitchen.

9. The cake is smelling great.

10. His father is outside. He washes his car.

11. His sister, Tina, is listen to music in her bedroom.

12. She is playing it too loud, and Alex is hearing it in the basement.

13. His sister, Sara, is plays a video game in the living room.

14. Everybody is seeming very happy.

C. Complete these sentences with the correct word or phrase.

15. School ____ at 8:30 every day, so why are you late?

    a. starts **b.** is starting **c.** start

16. Excuse me. ____ anyone sitting here?

    a. Do **b.** Is **c.** Does

17. Flight 103 ____ at 5:00 every evening, according to the schedule.

    a. is leaving **b.** does leave **c.** leaves

18. Please ____ the flowers.

    a. not pick **b.** not picking **c.** don't pick

19. Right now, I ____ a bath.

    a. am taking **b.** takes **c.** take

20. Excuse me, how many cars ____ in the garage? Is there room for mine?

    a. fits **b.** do fit **c.** fit

21. Bring the umbrella! It ____ outside.

    a. rains **b.** 's raining **c.** rain

22. ____ your parents come from El Salvador?

    a. Are **b.** Do **c.** Does

23. The sign says "Danger: ____ enter."

    a. No **b.** Do not **c.** Not

24. My father ____ like tomatoes.

    a. doesn't **b.** don't **c.** isn't

25. Eva ____ the furniture once a week.

    a. is dusting **b.** dust **c.** dusts

26. Don't take that truck, Ben. It ____ to you.

    a. doesn't belong **b.** don't belong **c.** isn't belonging

27. I speak Spanish, but I ____ it.

    a. not write **b.** not writing **c.** don't write

28. The post office is on 9th Avenue. ____ right at the corner.

    a. Turn **b.** Turning **c.** Turns

29. ____ smoke here, please.

    a. Don't **b.** No **c.** Not

30. Oh, no! Look at the scale! I ____ 150 pounds!

    a. am weighing **b.** weigh **c.** weighs

4 The Simple Past

FORM

1 Examining Form

Read this magazine article and complete the tasks below.

Robin Williams

Robin Williams, actor

Robin Williams <u>was</u> an only child. His parents were wealthy; his father was an executive at the Ford Motor Company. His mother was often busy. As a result, Robin ⬚spent⬚ a lot of time alone.

Robin was a good student. He ⭕admired his father and tried to please him by working hard in school. Mr. Williams believed in discipline and hard work.

Robin went to college to study politics and economics. But during his first year he took an acting class. He found that he loved the theater, and he was a good actor.

When Robin returned home after the spring semester, he nervously told his father that he wanted to be an actor. His father wasn't very happy. He advised his son to learn a more useful skill.

1. There are seven examples of the past tense forms of *be* in the article. The first one is underlined. Underline six more.

2. There are seven examples of regular simple past verbs in the article. The first one is circled. Circle six more.

3. There are five examples of irregular simple past verbs in the article (not including *be*). The first one is boxed. Draw a box around four more.

Working on the Simple Past of *Be*

Complete this paragraph with *was* and *were*.

It <u>was</u> a beautiful day in late August. The clouds _____
high in the sky. Best of all, the circus _____ in town. My brother and I
_____ very excited. This _____ something new for us. My
brother _____ interested in the elephants. They _____ old and
tired, but for him they _____ wonderful creatures.

Rewriting Statements in the Simple Past

Read what a student says about his favorite teacher and complete the task below.

Mr. Kennedy is a great teacher. He teaches me English. I learn a lot in his class. First, he explains things clearly. When two words have similar meanings, he shows us the difference in a simple way. Time goes by quickly in his class. We don't get bored.

Mr. Kennedy doesn't have favorites. He spends time with everyone. He doesn't make comments about the weaker students. He encourages them and helps them a lot. He knows everyone's name by the second class. He's everyone's favorite teacher, and he really enjoys teaching.

What did the student say a year later? Rewrite the paragraphs, changing the simple present verbs to the simple past.

_____ Mr. Kennedy was a great teacher. He taught me English . . . . _____

_____

_____

_____

_____

_____

Use the statements and the words in parentheses to write *Yes/No* questions.

1. I was born in Colombia.

(your brother?) <u>Was your brother born in Colombia?</u>

2. I was very happy in Colombia.

(your parents?) _____

3. I came to the U.S. in 1998.

(your parents?) _____

4. My mother wanted to move to the U.S.

(your father?) _____

5. I was very homesick at first.

(your sisters?) _____

6. My mother found work.

(your father?) _____

Use the words in parentheses to write information questions for the answers below. Use the simple past.

1. Alexander Fleming discovered penicillin.

   a. (Alexander Fleming) <u>Who discovered penicillin?</u>

   b. (penicillin) <u>What did Alexander Fleming discover?</u>

2. Leonardo da Vinci painted the *Mona Lisa*.

   a. (the *Mona Lisa*) _____

   b. (Leonardo da Vinci) _____

3. The California Gold Rush began in 1848.

   a. (the California Gold Rush) _____

   b. (in 1848) _____

4. Nelson Mandela won the Nobel Peace Prize in 1993.

   a. (Nelson Mandela) _____

   b. (in 1993) _____

MEANING AND USE

Read the sentences in the box about some events in one woman's life and complete the task below.

> **a.** As a child, Celia Clark was often sick for many months at a time.
>
> **b.** But every time her class had an exam, she got the best grade.
>
> **c.** She graduated from college on May 15, 1986.
>
> **d.** Last month she went to Peru.
>
> **e.** She got married last Sunday.

Match the events in Celia's life to the uses of the simple past. You may use a letter more than once.

1. an action or state in the distant past _a_ ___ ___

2. an action or state in the recent past ___ ___

3. an action or state that happened repeatedly ___ ___

4. an action or state that happened only once ___ ___ ___

Replace the underlined simple past verb forms with *used to* where appropriate and rewrite the sentences. In two sentences, *used to* is not appropriate. For these sentences, make no change.

1. My grandparents <u>had</u> a farm in Virginia.
   <u>My grandparents used to have a farm in Virginia.</u>

2. I <u>went</u> there every summer.
   _____

3. One summer my grandfather <u>asked</u> me to help him with work on the farm.
   _____

4. I <u>loved</u> working on the farm.
   _____

5. I <u>took</u> very good care of the animals.
   _____

6. One day my grandfather <u>taught</u> me to drive his tractor.
   _____

COMBINING FORM, MEANING, AND USE

8 Editing

There are twelve errors in this student's composition. The first one has been corrected. Find and correct eleven more.

> came
> I ~~come~~ to the United States two years ago, when I was 15 years old. I was sad when I left my home country, especially when I say good-bye to my friends.
>
> At the beginning, living in the U.S. isn't easy for me. In those days the language is hard for me because I don't speak it very well. Also, my parents don't speak English at all then, so I help them. A few months after I came here, I met some people who become my friends. This makes a big difference in my life at that time. After I meet them, I feel more confident.
>
> Now I am going to school, I had some friends, and my English is better, too.

9 Writing

A. Think about your first day in a new place—for example, in a new country or a new school. Take notes on the following questions and on other details you remember:

- What was the new place?
- When was this?
- Who were you with?
- Why were you there?

- What happened?
- What did you think?
- How did you feel?
- Who did you meet?

B. On a separate sheet of paper, write a paragraph about your first day in the new place. Use your notes, and put events in the correct order. Use the simple past.

> I remember the first day I went to my high school. I was still in eighth grade. My teacher took our class to the high school for a visit. . . .

5 The Past Continuous and Past Time Clauses

FORM

 Examining Form

Read this story and complete the task below.

Drama in the Air

It was impossible to sleep. The plane <u>was shaking</u> violently. The lights in the cabin were flashing, and the TV sets lost their pictures. 5 Something in the kitchen area fell to the floor with a loud crash. The flight attendant announced an emergency landing at Tokyo airport. Everybody was scared. A child was crying, and 10 some passengers were holding onto each other. I felt that the plane was going down, but I couldn't see anything because it was raining.

Fifteen minutes later, the plane 15 landed. I looked out the window. Ambulances and fire trucks were rushing toward us. When the plane finally came to a stop, the attendants opened all the emergency doors and 20 helped us get off the plane. Doctors were waiting to meet us. A few passengers had minor injuries, but I was OK. The next day, I took another plane to the United States.

There are eight examples of the past continuous in the story. The first one is underlined. Underline seven more.

2 **Working on the Past Continuous**

Rewrite these sentences, changing the simple past verbs to the past continuous.

1. Fumiko wore a red dress.

   <u>Fumiko was wearing a red dress</u> _____ when I met her.

2. We ate lunch in the cafeteria.

   _____ when we heard a crash in the kitchen.

3. You sat on the deck.

   _____ when I got here.

4. The sun shone.

   _____ when we left the house.

5. The boys walked to the park.

   _____ when it started to rain.

3 **Asking Information Questions**

Complete the conversation about a power blackout. Use the words and phrases to write information questions with the past continuous.

1. What / you / do / when the lights went out?

   Hector: <u>What were you doing when the lights went out?</u>

   Lisa: I was studying with a friend.

2. Who / you / study / with?

   Hector: _____

   Lisa: I was studying with Holly.

3. Where / you / study?

   Hector: _____

   Lisa: In the library.

4. Why / you / study?

   Hector: _____

   Lisa: Because we had an exam the next day.

5. Where / you / sit?

   Hector: _____

   Lisa: By the window.

Working on Past Time Clauses

Rewrite these sentences, changing the order of the clauses. Make changes as necessary.

1. When Amy looked out the window, she couldn't believe her eyes.

   Amy couldn't believe her eyes when she looked out the window.

2. We walked home after the rain stopped.

   _____

3. Keiko was exhausted when she got home.

   _____

4. After Hanna graduated from college, she moved to Los Angeles.

   _____

5. Paulo felt relaxed while he was on his vacation.

   _____

MEANING AND USE

5 **Understanding the Past Continuous and the Simple Past**

Choose the correct use of the past forms in each sentence.

1. We were watching TV when the lights went out.
   a. describes two simultaneous events
   b. describes one event interrupted by another

2. Last semester I was getting ready for an exam. My friend Holly and I were studying in the library. Suddenly...
   a. gives background information
   b. describes events in sequence

3. While I was eating, the phone rang.
   a. describes two simultaneous events
   b. describes one event interrupted by another

4. After Fred quit his job, he moved back to Ohio.
   a. describes one event interrupted by another
   b. describes events in sequence

5. Erica, I was thinking about you last night. I'm so glad you called.
   a. describes an activity in progress in the past
   b. gives background information

Choose the best answer to complete each sentence.

1. We went out to eat after _____.
   a. I finished my homework
   b. I was finishing my homework

2. While I was sleeping, _____.
   a. Paul was coming into the room
   b. Paul came into the room

3. I was living in Europe when _____.
   a. you grew up in New York City
   b. you were growing up in New York City

4. When we looked out the window, _____.
   a. it snowed
   b. it was snowing

5. _____ when I fell asleep.
   a. I was watching TV
   b. I watched TV

6. We opened the letter after _____.
   a. we received it
   b. we were receiving it

7. _____ when it cracked.
   a. Susan held the glass
   b. Susan was holding the glass

8. _____ when he fell.
   a. He was walking
   b. He walked

9. I was waiting at the airport when _____.
   a. I was hearing about the delay
   b. I heard about the delay

10. Ana left the party before _____.
    a. her sister came for her
    b. her sister was coming for her

Look at Bob's journal and complete the tasks below.

Wednesday, March 20

8:55-9:30: _Read e-mail (9:20: the boss arrived)_

9:30-10:00: _Prepared the conference room for a meeting_

10:00-11:00: _Took notes in the meeting_

11:00-11:15: _Made copies, then the copy machine broke_

11:15-12:10: _Made phone calls (11:30: received a fax from New York office, but the_
fax machine jammed)

12:10-1:00: _Went to lunch (12:30: boss in a meeting)_

A. Write **T** for *true* or **F** for *false* for each statement.

__F__ **1.** The boss arrived at work before Bob did.

_____ **2.** Bob was reading his e-mail when the boss arrived.

_____ **3.** Before the meeting, Bob prepared the conference room.

_____ **4.** Bob took notes before he prepared the conference room.

_____ **5.** He made copies before he took notes in the meeting.

_____ **6.** The copy machine broke after he made copies.

_____ **7.** Before Bob made phone calls, the fax machine jammed.

_____ **8.** The fax machine jammed after the copy machine broke.

_____ **9.** While Bob was at lunch, his boss was in a meeting.

_____ **10.** Bob went to lunch before he received a fax.

B. There are five false statements in part A. Rewrite the false statements as true statements. The first one has been done for you.

1. The boss arrived at work after Bob did.

_____

_____

_____

_____

_____

COMBINING FORM, MEANING, AND USE

8) Editing

There are six errors in this student's composition. The first one has been corrected. Find and correct five more.

> *was walking*
> While I ~~walked~~ home from the Chinatown library yesterday, a strange thing happened to me. When I was reaching the corner of Broadway and Stockton, I stopped because the light was red. I was waiting for the light to change, and suddenly someone was tapping me once on my shoulder. Who was it? I turned around to find out. A man were standing behind me. When the light changed, I began to walk really fast. But every time I looked behind me, I was seeing the man. Finally, I went into a drugstore to escape from him. Ten minutes later I was coming out. The man was still outside! He came up to me and spoke. "Are you Susie Lin?" he asked. "I'm your cousin from Vancouver."

9) Writing

On a separate sheet of paper, answer the questions below to write a one-paragraph mystery story. Use the simple past, the past continuous, and past time clauses. Use your imagination!

1. First, give the background information: What time was it? Where were you? Who were you with? What were you doing, talking about, or thinking?

2. Then describe the action: What happened suddenly? What did you do? What did you see? What happened then?

3. Finally, tell how your story ends.

> It was about nine o'clock on a Sunday evening. It was raining, and I was playing cards with my family. Suddenly, there was a loud noise outside the window. We ran to the window, and when we looked outside. . . .

6

The Present Perfect

FORM

1 Examining Form

Read this newspaper article and complete the tasks below.

Some Will Go the Extra Mile

Unlike most people, Marty O'Brien loves long car trips. In fact, he often tries to make them longer.

5   Marty is a member of the Extra Miler Club. His goal is to visit every one of the 3,145 counties in the United States. So far, he <u>has visited</u> 1,441. "On every trip," he says, "I 10 look for new places to go."

    That's the philosophy of the people in the Extra Miler Club. The club began in 1973, and it now has 207 members. Twelve of these 15 members have visited every county. They have even traveled by seaplane to get to counties in Alaska that are hard to reach. Some others have been to every state.

20   Roy Carson is one of the people who started the club. In 1985 he traveled to his last county. But he didn't take any photographs on his trips. So now he is trying again. 25 This time he is taking photographs of himself in front of each county sign. So far, he has covered 538,427 miles. "It's just as much fun the second time around, but it's a lot 30 more expensive," he says. Gas cost just 39 cents a gallon when he first started—in 1949.

---

county: a geographical and political division within a state in the U.S.

---

1. There are five examples of the present perfect in the article. The first one is underlined. Underline four more.

2. How is the present perfect formed? _____

Complete these questions with the past participles of the verbs in the box. Then answer the questions.

be	eat	find	fly	meet	ride

Have you ever . . .

1. _been_ on television? _No, I haven't._

2. _____ a horse? _____

3. _____ Indian food? _____

4. _____ a famous person? _____

5. _____ in a helicopter? _____

6. _____ money in the street? _____

3 **Asking Information Questions**

Use the words and phrases to write information questions in the present perfect.

1. How long / you / be / out of college?

   How long have you been out of college?

2. Where / you / travel / to?

   _____

3. How many people / she / invite?

   _____

4. Who / be / to China?

   _____

5. Why / you / choose / that book?

   _____

6. How long / Larry / live / there?

   _____

7. What / you / prepare / for lunch?

   _____

8. How much money / you / spend / this week?

   _____

MEANING AND USE

4) Understanding the Present Perfect

Choose the best answer to complete each sentence.

1. She's been a teacher all her life, _____.
   a. and she loved her job
   b. and she loves her job *(circled)*

2. I've traveled in Europe a lot, and in 2001 _____.
   a. I've gone to Africa
   b. I went to Africa

3. I've had that car for five years, _____.
   a. and it never breaks down
   b. and I sold it

4. We haven't eaten at the Greek restaurant yet, _____.
   a. so we tried it last night
   b. so we want to try it soon

5. We haven't solved the problem yet, _____.
   a. so we gave up
   b. but we aren't giving up

6. Pedro is one of my best friends; _____.
   a. I've known him for a long time
   b. I knew him for a long time

5) Using *For* and *Since*

Complete these time expressions and time clauses with *for* or *since*.

1. _for_____ three days

2. _____ 3 o'clock

3. _____ a long time

4. _____ a moment

5. _____ last month

6. _____ a month

7. _____ he was a boy

8. _____ 1988

Contrasting the Present Perfect and the Simple Past

Complete this conversation with the present perfect or simple past forms of the verbs in parentheses. Use contractions when possible.

A: Why do you want to work here?

B: Well, I _'ve loved_ (love) children all my life. I _____ (want) to work
$\quad\quad$ 1 $\quad\quad\quad\quad\quad\quad\quad\quad\quad\quad$ 2

with kids since I _____ (leave) high school.
$\quad\quad\quad\quad\quad\quad$ 3

A: Your resume says that you _____ (work) in the childcare center at the
$\quad\quad\quad\quad\quad\quad\quad\quad\quad\quad$ 4

university from 1999 to 2001. Can you tell me about that?

B: Yes. It _____ (be) a part-time job. We _____ (play) with the
$\quad\quad\quad$ 5 $\quad\quad\quad\quad\quad\quad\quad\quad\quad$ 6

children and _____ (give) them lunch. I _____ (work) with a
$\quad\quad\quad\quad\quad\quad$ 7 $\quad\quad\quad\quad\quad\quad\quad\quad$ 8

Head Teacher.

A: Tell me about the jobs you _____ (have) since then. _____ (you/
$\quad\quad\quad\quad\quad\quad\quad\quad\quad$ 9 $\quad\quad\quad\quad\quad\quad\quad\quad$ 10

ever have) full responsibility for children in your care?

B: Yes. For the last year I _____ (look after) one-year-old twins.
$\quad\quad\quad\quad\quad\quad\quad$ 11

Using Adverbs with the Present Perfect

Use the words below to rewrite each sentence in two ways. Do not change the meaning of the sentence. More than one answer may be possible.

1. I haven't seen a volcano in my whole life.

| already | never | still | so far | yet |

$\quad$ **a.** _I've never seen a volcano._

$\quad$ **b.** _I haven't seen a volcano yet._

2. Up to now, we've raised $5,700.

$\quad$ **a.** _____

$\quad$ **b.** _____

3. He hasn't been to Europe.

$\quad$ **a.** _____

$\quad$ **b.** _____

4. They've interviewed five people.

$\quad$ **a.** _____

$\quad$ **b.** _____

COMBINING FORM, MEANING, AND USE

8) Editing

There are nine errors in these paragraphs. The first one has been corrected. Find and correct eight more.

> ~~travel~~ traveled
> My wife and I have ~~travel~~ as much as possible since we retired. We've visited cousins in Australia, and we been to New Zealand twice. We've also went on safari in Africa. We've been to Europe a lot. Gina and I has spent time in Paris, in Madrid, and in several cities in Italy. We haven't to Eastern Europe yet, though. We hope to visit Prague and Budapest next year.
>
> My sister Betty was born in the United States, and she has never traveled outside the country—except once when she was very young. But she have been to a lot of places in the U.S. She has visit most of the national parks: the Grand Canyon, Yellowstone, Yosemite, and so on. She has been to all of the big cities, too. In fact, she is lived in four different cities in the U.S.: New York, Boston, Los Angeles, and San Francisco. I think she seen more of her own country than most people.

9) Writing

On a separate sheet of paper, write a paragraph about your travel experiences. Use the present perfect or the simple past as needed.

1. In your first few sentences, describe your travel experience in general.

2. In the rest of the paragraph, describe one or more trips in particular. Use the questions below to help you write your paragraph:
   - How many countries or cities have you visited?
   - Have you visited any places more than once?
   - Where did you go on a recent trip?
   - Think of places you haven't visited. Which ones would you like to visit?

> I haven't traveled very much outside my country, but I have visited different areas in my country. For example, I've been to Chiang Mai in northern Thailand several times. My last visit to Chiang Mai was last year. . . .

Chapters 4–6

A. Complete the sentences with the correct form of the verbs in the box.

| begin | bite | buy | eat | fall | fly | give | grow | hear | lose | say | sell | throw | wear |

1. Who _____ , "I have a dream" in 1963?

2. Myles _____ the ball, and Carl caught it.

3. Julie Morgan? Who was she? I've never _____ of her.

4. Amelia Earhart _____ a small plane across the Atlantic in 1932.

5. We went to the store and _____ everything for the party.

6. You're late! The movie has already _____ .

7. Our neighbors _____ their house and moved to Idaho.

8. Have you ever _____ frogs' legs?

9. I've never _____ this jacket before. Does it look OK?

10. She wasn't finished with the test, so we _____ her more time.

11. She hurt her knee when she _____ off her bike.

12. You're such a big girl! You've _____ a lot since the last time I saw you.

13. Ow! That dog _____ me!

14. Have you seen my keys? I've _____ them again.

B. Read these sentences. Check (✓) *OK* if the sentence is logical or *NOT OK* if the sentence is not logical.

	OK	NOT OK
15. Paul was a carpenter for ten years, and he loves it.		
16. We lived in Atlanta for five years.		
17. She's worked here for six years before she left in July.		
18. After I heard the news, I went straight to the hospital.		
19. While he was taking a shower, he got dressed.		
20. After I fell asleep, I read the newspaper.		
21. I haven't seen Lee since yesterday.		

C. Choose the correct word or phrase to complete each sentence.

22. How long _____ you been here?
    a. are   b. did   c. have

23. _____ you home last night?
    a. Are   b. Did   c. Were

24. After our guests _____, we sat down to dinner.
    a. arrived   b. were arriving   c. have arrived

25. Who _____ to when I saw you yesterday?
    a. you talk   b. are you talking   c. were you talking

26. Where have you been? I haven't seen you _____ a long time!
    a. at   b. for   c. since

27. We've _____ finished phase one of the project.
    a. already   b. still   c. yet

28. We _____ go there often when we were children, but we do now.
    a. used to   b. didn't use   c. didn't use to

29. My father _____ Silvio since they were kids.
    a. knows   b. has known   c. knew

30. We were all very upset _____ we heard the bad news.
    a. during   b. when   c. while

7 Future Time: *Be Going To, Will,* and the Present Continuous

---

FORM

 Examining Form

Read this letter and complete the tasks below.

To: Lisa Miller
From: Jada Hal
Cc: Gina Flynn
Subject: New address

---

5 Hi everyone!

Great news! Luisa and I have found an apartment! We're moving in next Saturday. My new address <u>will be</u>:

235 New St. #6
Berkeley, CA 94703

10 It's a really nice apartment. It's small, but it's really close to campus, so we can walk to school. It's a little more expensive than we expected, but we won't need to take the bus, so we'll save some money there. We'll also save money by eating at home more. I'm looking forward to having our own place. I'm sure Luisa will be a great roommate. She's (going to cook,) and I'm going to clean. It's all arranged!

15 We don't have a lot of furniture, but Luisa's brother is going to give us some of his old furniture, so we'll be all set. He's going to help us move, too!

Anyway, I have to go now. I'll write again soon.

Love,
Jada

---

1. There are four examples of the future with *be going to* in the letter. The first one is circled. Circle three more.

2. There are seven examples of the future with *will* in the letter. The first one is underlined. Underline six more. One of the examples is negative.

3. There is one example of the present continuous as future. Draw a box around it.

2 Working on Statements and Questions with *Be Going To*

Use the words and phrases to write conversations with *be going to*. Use contractions when possible.

Conversation 1

1. **Jenny:** we / get married in the spring.

   <u>We're going to get married in the spring.</u>

2. **Ana:** you / have a big wedding?

   _____

3. **Jenny:** No. We / not / have a big celebration.

   _____

Conversation 2

4. **Myles:** it / rain tomorrow?

   _____

5. **Eric:** Yes. What / you / do?

   _____

6. **Myles:** I / stay home and read a book.

   _____

3 Asking Information Questions with *Will*

Write information questions about the underlined phrases. Use *will*.

1. <u>Where will you meet me?</u>

   I'll meet you <u>at the tennis courts</u>.

2. _____

   He'll find out the results <u>on Tuesday</u>.

3. _____

   We'll go <u>to the movies</u>.

4. _____

   <u>Ms. Santiago</u> will be there.

5. _____

   The photos will be ready <u>at noon</u>.

6. _____

   It will take <u>almost four hours</u>.

Read what Gary's friend says about Gary's daily routine and complete the task below.

> My friend Gary has never heard of the expression "Variety is the spice of life."
> Every day Gary gets up at 6:00, puts on shorts and a T-shirt, and goes out for a run.
> He gets back at 6:45, takes a shower, and shaves. He goes downstairs at 7:00. He
> makes a cup of coffee, but he doesn't drink it. He takes it with him in his car. He
> doesn't eat anything, either. Then he drives to work. He has breakfast at his desk.

If Gary does the same things every day, what will he do tomorrow? Rewrite the paragraph, using *will*. Use contractions when possible.

_____ My friend Gary will get up at 6:00, put on shorts and a T-shirt, and go
out for a run.
_____
_____
_____
_____

MEANING AND USE

5 **Understanding *Will***

A. Match each statement to a place or situation.

  _d_ **1.** I won't tell Mom.

  ___ **2.** This will hurt a little.

  ___ **3.** I'll have the steak.

  ___ **4.** I'll buy that one.

  ___ **5.** I'll give her the message.

  ___ **6.** Rain showers will begin this evening.

a. on the phone

b. on TV or the radio

c. in a store

d. at home

e. at the doctor's office

f. in a restaurant

B. How is each statement in part A used? Write the number of the statement next to the appropriate use below.

a. a promise: _1_ ____

b. a prediction: ____ ____

c. a decision: ____ ____

Read this conversation and complete the tasks below.

Larry: Are you and Kate having a good vacation here in Colorado?

Paul: We're having a wonderful time. It's so nice here. We don't want to go home.

Larry: When are you leaving?

Paul: Next week. We're leaving here on Wednesday. Then we're flying home on Sunday.

Larry: Where are you going in between?

Paul: We're going to visit some friends in Boulder for a few days.

Larry: Well, come for dinner before you leave. What are you doing tomorrow?

Paul: I think we're going to hike up the mountain.

Larry: Really? Are you sure? They say the weather's going to be bad. You're going to get very wet. Why don't you spend the day with Julie and me in Aspen instead?

Write the questions and statements from the conversation that show the following uses:

1. *be going to* to talk about future plans or intentions

   a. <u>We're going to visit some friends in Boulder for a few days.</u>

   b. _____

2. *be going to* to make predictions

   a. _____

   b. _____

3. the present continuous to talk about future plans or intentions

   a. _____

   b. _____

   c. _____

   d. _____

   e. _____

4. the present continuous to talk about the present

   a. _____

   b. _____

7 **Contrasting *Be Going To* and the Present Continuous**

Look at these pairs of sentences. Write *S* if they have the same meaning. Write *D* if their meanings are different.

1. __D__ What are you doing?

   What are you going to do?

2. _____ We're getting married next month.

   We're going to get married next month.

3. _____ She's losing weight.

   She's going to lose weight.

4. _____ We're not going on vacation this year.

   We're not going to go on vacation this year.

5. _____ Are you working this evening?

   Are you going to work this evening?

6. _____ My boss is getting mad at me.

   My boss is going to get mad at me.

COMBINING FORM, MEANING, AND USE

8 **Thinking About Meaning and Use**

Choose the correct sentence to complete each conversation.

1. **A:** What are your plans for summer vacation?

   B: _____

   a. I'll spend a month in Hawaii.

   b. I'm going to spend a month in Hawaii.

2. **A:** What are you guys doing this afternoon?

   B: _____

   a. We'll play tennis.

   b. We're going to play tennis.

3. **A:** Oh, no! That's the phone.

   B: _____

   a. I'll get it.

   b. I'm going to get it.

4. **A:** I want to sell my sofa.

   B: _____

   a. I'll give you $30 for it.

   b. I'm giving you $30 for it.

5. **A:** Why are you buying a German dictionary?

   B: _____

   a. I'll study German.

   b. I'm going to study German.

6. **A:** What time do you leave?

   B: _____

   a. I'll take the 5:00 bus.

   b. I'm taking the 5:00 bus.

A. Imagine you are taking a trip to Egypt next week. Read the itinerary below.

B. On a separate sheet of paper, write a one-paragraph e-mail to a friend about the trip. Using information from the itinerary, tell about your plans and make some predictions. Express future time with the present continuous and *will* as appropriate.

Globe Travel • 202 Sanford Avenue • Newark, NJ 07039

Travel Itinerary

Day 1 – Saturday	Leave the U.S. for Europe.
Day 2 – Sunday	Arrive in Frankfurt. Leave that evening for Cairo. On arrival, we take you to your hotel.
Day 3 – Monday	Cairo. Get up early for a visit to the Pyramids and the Egyptian Museum. In the afternoon, take a drive through Old Cairo.
Day 4 – Tuesday	Cairo/Nile Cruise. Fly to the Aswan Dam and board your cruise ship.
Days 5-8 – Wednesday-Saturday	Nile Cruise. See beautiful views of the River Nile. Visit old temples during the day and relax on the boat at night.
Day 9 – Sunday	Return to Cairo.
Day 10 – Monday	Fly back to the U.S.

To: Kevin Ross
From: Paul Lee
Cc:
Subject: Trip to Egypt

Hi Kevin,

I'm going on a ten-day trip to Egypt! We're leaving on Saturday and flying into Frankfurt.

Sunday morning. . . .

8 Future Time Clauses and *If* Clauses

FORM

Read the article and complete the tasks below.

A Polish Tradition

All parents wonder about their children's future. Will the infant sleeping peacefully in her crib become a doctor, a teacher, or a 5 future president? Many Polish families follow an old tradition to determine what kind of person their child will turn into. On the child's first birthday, the parents set several 10 objects on a table. For example, they may set out a book, a piece of bread, a set of car keys, and a musical instrument. They then sit the child at the table. Which object will 15 the child touch first?

If the child touches the book, she will be a good student. If the child reaches for the car keys, he will travel far. If the child goes for the 20 bread, she will love food. And if he touches the musical instrument, he will become a musician, of course!

---

1. Underline the main clauses in the second paragraph. What tense is used?

_____

2. What tense is used in the dependent (future/*if*) clauses? _____

Use the words or phrases to complete each sentence with a future time clause or a main clause. Use contractions when possible.

1. (if / I / finish / work early) <u>If I finish work early</u> _____, I'll go to a movie.

2. (we / eat / dinner) _____ when your father gets home.

3. Before I pay any more bills, _____ (I / cash / my paycheck).

4. Mr. Owens is going to retire _____ (when / he / turn / 68).

5. (I / not be / upset) _____ if you tell me the truth.

6. After the game is over, _____ (we / celebrate).

7. (I / buy / a new car) _____ if I get a raise.

8. (if / you / drive / too fast) _____, you'll have an accident.

Rewrite these sentences, changing the order of the clauses. Use correct punctuation.

1. We're going to go shopping tonight if the stores stay open.

   <u>If the stores stay open, we're going to go shopping tonight.</u>

2. After I say good-bye to the children, I'll be ready to leave.

   _____

3. Sun-hee will be angry if we don't invite Eric to the party.

   _____

4. We're going to pick up the car when Victor gets here.

   _____

5. If the water's too cold, I'm not going to go swimming.

   _____

6. Dinner will be ready when the guests arrive.

   _____

7. They'll buy a bigger house if they have another baby.

   _____

8. After I graduate, I'll look for a job in San Francisco.

   _____

MEANING AND USE

4 **Understanding Future Time Clauses and *If* Clauses**

Complete these sentences with future time clauses, *if* clauses, or main clauses.

1. _I will be very happy_ when I finish this course.

2. I will study for the test before _____.

3. I will see my family when _____.

4. I will get a job after _____.

5. _____ if you help me study.

6. I will go on vacation if _____.

7. Before the day is over _____.

8. After I finish this exercise _____.

5 **Understanding *If* Clauses**

Read the sentences in the box. How is each one used? Write the letter of each sentence next to the appropriate use below.

> **a.** I'll call you if I get an answer.
>
> **b.** If you don't hurry up, you're going to miss the train.
>
> **c.** You won't get sick if you drink lots of water.
>
> **d.** If you wait here, I'll introduce you to Nesha.
>
> **e.** If Kane wins the election, he'll be a good mayor.
>
> **f.** They won't let you in if you don't have your card.
>
> **g.** If you ask the driver, he'll tell you when to get off.
>
> **h.** If it gets colder, it will probably snow.

1. a prediction: _e_ _____

2. a promise: _____ _____

3. a warning: _____ _____

4. advice: _____ _____

Understanding Events in Sequence

Choose the correct sentence to complete each conversation.

1. **Betty:** This coat might not go on sale.

   Kedra: _____

   ⓐ Well, if it goes on sale, I'll buy it.

   b. Well, when it goes on sale, I'll buy it.

2. **Hiro:** We're definitely coming this evening.

   Eva: _____

   a. If you come, I'll introduce you to my parents.

   b. When you come, I'll introduce you to my parents.

3. **Mark:** If we take a trip to the beach next week, do you want to come?

   Tomek: _____

   a. When will you decide about the trip?

   b. When did you decide about the trip?

4. **Rick:** _____

   Gina: Thanks! I'll be ready.

   a. If I go to work tomorrow, I'll give you a ride.

   b. When I go to work tomorrow, I'll give you a ride.

COMBINING FORM, MEANING, AND USE

Thinking About Meaning and Use

Combine each pair of sentences, using the words in parentheses. Make any necessary changes. Use correct punctuation. More than one answer is possible.

1. I'll see you tomorrow. Then I'll give you the book. (when)

   When I see you tomorrow, I'll give you the book.

   OR I'll give you the book when I see you tomorrow.

2. Reiko will do well in the interview. Then she'll get the job. (if)

   _____

3. I'm going to join a gym. Then I'm going to lose ten pounds. (after)

   _____

4. The movie will end. Then I'll call you. (when)

   _____

5. We'll make too much noise. Then the baby will wake up. (if)

_____

6. We're going to eat dinner. Then we'll listen to the radio. (before)

_____

7. Matt will buy the groceries. Then he will go to the bank. (after)

_____

8. Ana will read more books. Then she will increase her vocabulary. (if)

_____

8 **Writing**

Read about Elena's situation and complete the task below.

Elena is 25 years old. She lives at home with her parents. She has lived in the same town all her life, and she has a lot of friends there. She works 40 hours a week in an office. The job pays a good salary, but it's boring. She probably won't be able to get a better job in her small town.

A large company in a city has offered Elena a job. It's a much better job: It's more interesting, and it pays more. But it will also be more stressful. Elena will have to leave home and find an apartment in a city where she doesn't know anyone. Elena isn't sure if she should take the job.

Imagine you are Elena. On a separate sheet of paper, write a two- or three-paragraph letter to a friend to describe different possibilities and predictions about your situation. What will happen if you stay at your old job? What will happen if you take the new job? Use _if_ clauses or future time clauses when possible.

Dear Yuji,

I was offered a job in the city, but I'm not sure what to do. If I stay at my old job, I will be close to my family... .

Chapters 7–8

A. Find and correct the error in each of these sentences.

1. I'll meeting John after work.

2. We not going to Los Angeles this summer.

3. I have an idea: I'm pick you up on my way to the airport.

4. Can you turn off the light after you are leaving the room?

5. Will you being at the party tomorrow?

6. When she will arrive home, she will phone her mother.

7. I going to tell you something.

8. This test isn't being easy.

B. Complete each response.

9. **Eva:** When are you going out?

   Paul: After _____ .

   a. I'll finish my homework
   b. I finish my homework

10. **Sasha:** Why are you still here'?

    Hector: I need to finish my work before _____ .

    a. I'm going home
    b. I go home

11. **Kim:** I'm going to bake a cake for the party.

    Sam: _____ , I'll make some cookies.

    a. If you bake a cake
    b. If you baked a cake

12. **Sandra:** I'm not feeling well.

    Ann: You'll feel better _____ .

    a. if you lie down
    b. if you're going to lie down

13. **Lee:** I think we're going to be late.

    Kedra: Well, if we leave now, _____ .

    a. we'll be on time
    b. we are on time

14. **Rita:** It's going to rain. You'll get wet!

    Nesha: If it rains, _____ .

    a. I used my umbrella
    b. I'll use my umbrella

15. **Maria:** Is Megan coming with us?

    Bill: Yes, _____ .

    a. if we drive there
    b. if we drove there.

16. **Keiko:** I'm going to the meeting now.

    Ana: Wait, _____ with you.

    a. I come
    b. I'll come

C. Choose the correct word or phrase to complete each sentence.

17. What _____ to do when you graduate?
    a. are you going   **b.** are going   **c.** you are going

18. If you take vitamins every day, you _____ get sick.
    a. aren't   **b.** not going to   **c.** won't

19. Have you heard the news? Tony and Diane _____ married!
    a. get   **b.** getting   **c.** are getting

20. The phone's ringing. I _____ it if you want.
    a. answer   **b.** 'll answer   **c.** 'm going to answer

21. I'll give Ms. Baxter the message when she _____ back.
    a. comes   **b.** will come   **c.** is going to come

22. If you don't drive more slowly, you _____ an accident.
    a. have   **b.** are having   **c.** are going to have

23. What _____ when they find out?
    a. your parents say   **b.** will your parents say   **c.** are your parents saying

24. I know it's a secret. Don't worry, I _____ a word.
    a. don't say   **b.** won't say   **c.** 'm not saying

25. I won't be home for dinner. I _____ with some people from school.
    a. 'm going out   **b.** go out   **c.** 'll go out

26. If you guys _____ that window, your father will be furious.
    a. break   **b.** will break   **c.** are breaking

27. If it breaks, I _____ you.
    a. call   **b.** 'll call   **c.** called

28. If you put on a hat, you _____ cold.
    a. aren't getting   **b.** not getting   **c.** won't get

29. I can't wait! I _____ on vacation next week.
    a. 'll be   **b.** being   **c.** be

30. Where _____ in Paris?
    a. you'll be   **b.** you are   **c.** will you be

9 Modals of Ability and Possibility

FORM

1 Examining Form

Miguel is planning a surprise birthday party for his friend Rosa, and Kalin is helping him. Read this e-mail that Miguel sent Kalin, and complete the tasks below.

To: Kalin Jones
From: Miguel Ortiz
Cc:
Subject: Rosa's birthday party

Hi Kalin,

I reserved a private room at Charlie's Restaurant for Rosa's surprise birthday party on Thursday.

The restaurant has two dining rooms, but I <u>couldn't</u> get the larger room because it was already

reserved. The manager said that the other room can hold around 25 people, so it will be large

5 enough.

I've already talked with some of Rosa's friends. Most said they will come. Carlos and Alex may

come, but they aren't sure. Kim is out of town, and she probably won't be back in time for the party.

Can you help me with a few more things before Thursday? I might not have time to do them. For

example, can you order the birthday cake? There could be a lot of people, so order a large cake.

10 Thanks a lot,

Miguel

---

1. There are ten examples of modals in the e-mail. The first one is underlined.
    Underline nine more.

2. Check the correct statement. Correct the incorrect statement.

    _____ Each modal has only one form.

    _____ Modals agree with the subject.

2 Working on Modals of Present and Past Ability

A. Rewrite these sentences, using *can*. Make all the necessary changes.

1. My father speaks Russian.

   My father can speak Russian.

2. I don't ski.

   _____

3. Do you drive?

   _____

4. They play several instruments.

   _____

B. Rewrite these sentences, using *could*. Make all the necessary changes.

1. We didn't see anything.

   _____

2. Did you play the piano when you were younger?

   _____

3. They didn't tell me anything.

   _____

4. Did Tomek understand that?

   _____

3 Working on Modals of Future Possibility

A. Use the words and phrases to write information questions with *could*.

1. **Emily:** Let's go somewhere tomorrow.

   Steve: OK. Where / go?

   Where could we go?

2. **Miguel:** Let's ask Young-soo to pick us up in his car.

   Sara: When / get here?

   _____

3. **Pedro:** It will take some time.

   Teresa: How long / take?

   _____

4. **Gary:** I hope nothing goes wrong.

   Hanna: What / go wrong?

   _____

B. Use the words and phrases to write information questions with *will.*

   1. **Victor:** I'm going to buy a new car.

      Megan: What kind / get?

      _____

   2. **Rita:** I don't have much money this month.

      Susan: How / pay / your rent?

      _____

   3. **Tony:** Steve's leaving for Las Vegas this morning.

      Kevin: What time / get / there?

      _____

   4. **Julie:** I'm meeting some friends at the restaurant.

      Gary: Who / be / there?

      _____

MEANING AND USE

4 Using Modals of Future Ability

Complete these sentences with *can/can't* or *will be able to/won't be able to.*

1. If I work on this for the next two months, maybe I _'ll be able to_ understand it.

2. People _____ travel great distances in outer space now, but

   maybe in the future they _____.

3. We _____ go to a restaurant this evening if you want to eat out.

4. The post office down the street is closing next month, so we _____

   go there much longer.

5. After the operation, you _____ see very well for a few days. But

   you _____ see much better in a few weeks.

6. When the new bridge opens, we _____ drive to the city in less

   than an hour.

5 Understanding Modals of Past Ability

Do these sentences about the past use *could* correctly? Check (✓) *Correct* or *Incorrect*.
Then correct the incorrect sentences with *be able to*.

	CORRECT	INCORRECT
1. After he talked to her, he ~~could~~ *was able to* find out what was wrong.		✓
2. I could feel the excitement in the room as soon as I walked in.		
3. She failed the exam the first time, but after she studied she could pass.		
4. We couldn't see a thing when we arrived at the top.		
5. They could visit Lee in the hospital yesterday.		

6 Understanding Modals of Future Possibility

Read these sentences about Keiko's evening. Then write each boldfaced action in the
correct column of the chart.

1. Keiko will **go out tonight.**

2. She'll **eat dinner.**

3. Maybe she will **study English.**

4. She may **read a book.**

5. She could **watch TV.**

6. She'll **go to bed before midnight.**

	LESS CERTAINTY	MORE CERTAINTY
1.		go out tonight
2.		
3.		
4.		
5.		
6.		

COMBINING FORM, MEANING, AND USE

7 **Thinking About Meaning and Use**

Complete these sentences with the correct modals.

1. When I was younger, I _____ understand a lot of Italian.

   a. can   **(b.)** could   **c.** might

2. We _____ get the tickets yesterday because Kevin waited in line for three hours.

   a. can   **b.** were able to   **c.** will be able to

3. I'm not sure where Dan will be tomorrow. He _____ be in London.

   a. can   **b.** may   **c.** will

4. He doesn't know much English now, but after he lives in the United States for a few months, he _____ understand much more.

   a. can   **b.** was able to   **c.** will be able to

5. Now you _____ buy stamps from ATM machines.

   a. can   **b.** might   **c.** may

6. It was dark when we arrived, so we _____ see anything.

   a. can't   **b.** couldn't   **c.** may not

8 **Writing**

A. Think about how transportation will be different in the future. Think about the following topics:

- crowded roads
- bicycles and motorcycles
- electric cars and buses
- high-speed trains
- space travel

B. On a separate sheet of paper, write a paragraph that describes how transportation might be different 50 years from now. Use some of these modals: *will/may/might/could/be able to.*

> Transportation could be very different 50 years from now. There will be a lot more people, especially in the cities. For that reason, public transportation might be... .

10 Modals and Phrases of Request, Permission, Desire, and Preference

FORM

1 **Examining Form**

Read these sentences from three telephone conversations and complete the tasks below.

> _C_ 1. "Express Air. <u>May</u> I help you?"
>
> _____ 2. "Could you hold on a minute? I'll check the fares."
>
> _____ 3. "He's not home yet. Can I take a message?"
>
> _____ 4. "What would you like to drink?"
>
> _____ 5. "Would you prefer to fly on a weekend?"
>
> _____ 6. "I'd like to change my order."
>
> _____ 7. "Can I speak to Paolo, please?"
>
> _____ 8. "I'd prefer the crispy noodles with that."
>
> _____ 9. "Could you tell him I called?"
>
> _____ 10. "I'd rather fly into London if that's possible."

1. Match the sentences above to _Conversations A, B,_ or _C_:
   - _Conversation A:_ Someone is ordering food from a restaurant.
   - _Conversation B:_ Someone is taking a message.
   - _Conversation C:_ Someone is talking with an airline representative about a flight reservation.

2. Underline the modal or phrase of request, permission, desire, or preference in each sentence.

Making Requests and Asking for Permission

Use the words to write questions. Use correct punctuation.

1. you / take / could / suitcases / those

   Could you take those suitcases?

2. I / coffee / more / some / have / may

   _____

3. you / take / would / picture / my

   _____

4. when / see / could / I / tomorrow / you

   _____

5. have / I / can / eat / something / to

   _____

6. me / you / will / give / a / ride

   _____

Working on *Would Like*, *Would Prefer*, and *Would Rather*

Rewrite these sentences using the words in parentheses. Make other changes and add *not* as necessary. Keep the meaning the same. Use contractions when possible.

1. Do you want to stay home tonight? (would rather)

   Would you rather stay home tonight?

2. I don't want to take a class on Fridays. (would prefer)

   _____

3. What time does Takeshi want to leave? (would like)

   _____

4. My mother doesn't want to come with us. (would rather)

   _____

5. Do you want milk or juice? (would prefer)

   _____

6. I want to live in a big city. (would like)

   _____

MEANING AND USE

4 **Understanding Modals of Request and Permission**

Rewrite each request in two ways for the situations given. Use the modals *can, would,* and *may.* More than one answer may be possible for each.

1. I'd like to speak with Carol.

   a. You're calling Carol at home: <u>Can I speak with Carol?</u>

   b. You're calling Carol at work: <u>May I speak with Carol, please?</u>

2. I'd like to talk to you after class.

   a. You say this to your classmate: _____

   b. You say this to your teacher: _____

3. Say that again.

   a. You say this to your brother: _____

   b. You say this to a stranger: _____

4. Drop me off at the corner.

   a. You say this to the bus driver: _____

   b. You say this to your friend: _____

5 **Understanding Desires, Requests, Offers, and Preferences**

Complete the conversations with *would like, would prefer,* and *would rather.* Use contractions when possible. More than one answer may be possible.

At home

Stefan: <u>Would</u> you <u>rather</u> stay home or go out to dinner tonight?

Irina: I think I _____ to go out rather than stay at home. How about you?

Stefan: I _____ go out, too. We could go to our favorite Chinese restaurant or try that new Italian restaurant.

Irina: I think tonight I _____ to try the Italian restaurant.

At the restaurant

Waiter: _____ you _____ some dessert now?

Irina: Yes, I _____ the cheesecake, please.

Waiter: And you, sir. _____ you _____ to have the cheesecake or the ice cream?

Stefan: I'm not having dessert. Thank you. But I _____ the check, please.

COMBINING FORM, MEANING, AND USE

Choose the correct word or phrase to complete each sentence.

1. May I _____ you?
   a. help   b. to help   c. helping

2. I don't have any money. _____ lend me five dollars?
   a. May you   b. Would you   c. Would you rather

3. A: May we use dictionaries?

   B: Yes, you _____ .
   a. may   b. could   c. would

4. A: Could you drive me home this evening?

   B: I'd like to, but I _____ .
   a. can't   b. couldn't   c. won't

5. A: _____ a cup of coffee?

   B: Yes, please.
   a. Would you rather   b. Do you like   c. Would you like

6. A: Would you let me know when it's ready?

   B: Yes, I _____ .
   a. would   b. will   c. can

7. I'd prefer _____ .
   a. stay home   b. to stay home   c. stayed home

8. A: Would you like to leave early or stay late?

   B: I'd _____ leave early.
   a. like   b. prefer   c. rather

9. A: Who got the job?

   B: I _____ say.
   a. wouldn't rather   b. would rather not   c. had rather not

10. Would you rather _____ now?
    a. not leave   b. not to leave   c. don't leave

Imagine that you need to change your work schedule because you want to take a computer course. On a separate sheet of paper, write two notes, one to your boss, Kedra, and one to your co-worker, Won-joon.

1. In your note to Kedra, request the schedule change and say when you want to work and why.

2. In your note to Won-joon, ask him to work for you next Tuesday. That's the day you have to register for the class. Ask him to call you at home if he can't do it.

Include some of these modals and modal phrases: *can, could, would, may, would prefer, would rather* and *would like.* Make sure that your note to Kedra is more formal than your note to Won-joon.

Dear Kedra,

I would like to change my schedule in a couple of weeks because... .

Hi Won-joon,

Can you work for me next Tuesday? ... .

11 Modals and Phrasal Modals of Advice, Necessity, and Prohibition

FORM

1) Examining Form

Read this magazine article and complete the tasks below.

Weird and Wonderful Hobbies

Many people these days are collecting everything and anything. And they're having fun doing it.

What (should) you collect? The
5 answer depends on your interests. You could collect old magazines, postcards, toys, buttons, posters, dolls… . The list is endless. But if you're going to start collecting
10 something, there are a few points you must consider. First, you should try to focus on one specific area of interest. For example, bottle collecting is a popular hobby. But
15 you'd better choose one special kind of bottle to collect, or your house will be full of glass in no time.

Next, you should learn
20 everything you can about your hobby. This way you won't waste time or money collecting worthless items. For example, if you collect old postcards, you ought to know
25 that of the millions of postcards from before 1914, only about five percent are worth anything. If you want to be a successful collector, you have to know how to recognize
30 the valuable ones.

Finally, don't let money be your main reason for collecting. Collecting should be fun and educational, just like any other
35 hobby.

1. There are nine examples of modals and phrasal modals of advice and necessity in the article. The first one is circled. Circle eight more.

2. Underline the verb that goes with each modal.

Complete these sentences with *go* or *to go*.

1. I think we should _go_ to Janet's party.

2. We have _____ to work before 7:00.

3. You've got _____ to bed right now.

4. You'd better not _____ there too early.

5. Amy should _____ to school today.

6. We really must _____ right now.

7. Josh has _____ to the doctor in the morning.

8. The children ought _____ swimming tomorrow.

9. You'd better _____ now.

10. Celia's got _____ home for dinner.

Write information questions about the underlined words.

1. We have to buy <u>a present</u>.

   What do we have to buy?

2. She should tell <u>a teacher</u>.

   _____

3. They have to leave <u>next week</u>.

   _____

4. I have to stay <u>for an hour</u>.

   _____

5. He has to tell her <u>soon</u>.

   _____

6. Emily should do <u>something</u>.

   _____

7. You should ask <u>Celia</u>.

   _____

8. We should exercise <u>every day</u>.

   _____

Choose the correct word or phrase to complete each sentence.

1. You _____ let the baby put that in his mouth.

   a. couldn't   **b.** shouldn't

2. What kind of gift _____ get for my girlfriend?

   a. ought I   **b.** should I

3. We _____ get up early tomorrow.

   a. doesn't have to   **b.** don't have to

4. When do you _____ be at the airport?

   a. have to   **b.** must

5. You _____ to eat more vegetables.

   a. had better   **b.** ought

6. _____ to call my parents.

   a. I must   **b.** I've got

MEANING AND USE

Read this conversation. There are five examples of errors with modals and phrasal modals. The first one has been corrected. Find and correct four more. Some errors can be corrected in more than one way.

Satomi: I'm a little nervous about coming to the United States for the first time. What

   happens at the airport?

   has to/has got to

Chris: Well, everybody who is coming in from overseas had better go through

   Customs and Immigration. You could show your passport and your visa.

Satomi: OK. And how do I get from the airport to the university?

Chris: Well, you have to take public transportation, but it's probably better to take

   a taxi.

Satomi: How much will that cost?

Chris: About $30. But you might add a tip for the taxi driver. That's my advice—

   almost everyone tips. We usually tip about 15 percent.

Satomi: I see. What about money? What's the best way to keep my money?

Chris: Well, you could use traveler's checks, or you must open a bank account.

6) Using Modals and Phrasal Modals of Necessity and Prohibition

Complete the paragraph using modals and phrasal modals of necessity and prohibition.

Welcome to English 101. My name is Lisa Rosado, and I'll be your teacher.

Let me tell you a few things about the course. You _don't have to_ take notes right
now. Just listen carefully.

First, you _____ attend class regularly. If you want credit for this course,
you _____ miss more than six classes. You _____ come on time,
too.

You _____ complete all the homework assignments. For informal
assignments, handwriting is OK. You _____ type them. But you
_____ type formal assignments. And there are two exams. You
_____ pass these to pass the course.

You _____ have a dictionary for this class, but it's a very good idea.
Does anyone have any questions?

COMBINING FORM, MEANING, AND USE

7) Thinking About Meaning and Use

Choose the correct sentence to complete each conversation.

1. **A:** I'd like to learn how to dance.

   B: _____
   a. You must take some lessons.
   b. Maybe you should take some lessons.

2. **A:** Should I get some milk?

   B: _____ We still have enough.
   a. You don't need to.
   b. You must not.

3. **A:** I've got a bad sore throat and I feel terrible.

   B: _____
   a. You might go to bed early tonight.
   b. You'd better go to bed early tonight.

4. A: The car broke down on the way home.

  B: Not again! _____

    a. We could get a new car.

    b. We've got to get a new car.

5. A: What's a good way to lose weight?

  B: _____

    a. Well, you could join an exercise class.

    b. Well, you must not join an exercise class.

6. A: Can I come back for the blood test tomorrow morning?

  B: Yes. _____

    a. But you must not eat for 12 hours before the test.

    b. But you don't have to eat for 12 hours before the test.

8) **Writing**

On a separate sheet of paper, use the information below to write a one-paragraph letter. Give Bob your advice. Should he finish college now? Or should he take a year off? Use modals of advice and necessity in affirmative and negative statements.

Your friend Bob is thinking about dropping out of college. He has only one more year before he gets his degree, but he is bored with his classes. He wants to take a year off and then go back and finish his degree. However, his parents have told him that they won't pay for him to go back to college if he drops out now. He will have to pay for his own education.

> Dear Bob,
>
>   I really think that you should stay in school until you
>
> get your degree. You've got to think about your future. . . .

Chapters 9–11

A. Choose the correct clause to complete each sentence.

1. I can't go out for dinner _____.
   a. because it's a special occasion
   b. because I don't have any money

2. I'd better go out for dinner _____.
   a. because there isn't any food at home
   b. because I'm on a diet

3. I'd better not go out for dinner _____.
   a. because it's expensive
   b. because it's a special occasion

4. I'd like to go out for dinner _____.
   a. because it's expensive
   b. because it's a special occasion

5. I don't have to go out for dinner _____.
   a. if I don't want to
   b. because I'm on a diet

6. I'd rather go out for dinner _____.
   a. because it's expensive
   b. because I don't cook well

B. Rewrite these sentences, making them negative. Use contractions when possible.

7. It might rain.

   _____

8. I'd like to be in his situation.

   _____

9. He has to do it.

   _____

10. We'd better go now.

    _____

11. They'd prefer to wait.

    _____

12. She should leave.

    _____

13. He may come.

    _____

C. Find and correct the errors in these sentences.

14. It's really late. We really should to go home.

15. You don't have got to worry about dinner. Rosa has agreed to cook.

16. Yesterday I could run a mile in less than six minutes.

17. They would not rather work late tonight.

18. Where would you like go to college?

19. It's a long way to the station. I'd prefer to drive rather walk.

20. Susan might helps with our math homework.

21. When we lived in Africa, we can see elephants and giraffes.

D. Choose *two* words or phrases to complete each sentence.

22. _____ you give me a hand?

    a. Can   **b.** Could   **c.** May

23. Take an umbrella. It _____ rain later.

    a. can   **b.** could   **c.** might

24. Sorry I'm late. I _____ find a parking space.

    a. couldn't   **b.** may not   **c.** wasn't able to

25. I don't know where she is. She _____ be at work.

    a. can   **b.** may   **c.** might

26. My parents are probably getting worried now. I _____ go home.

    a. 'd better   **b.** could   **c.** should

27. If I don't wear my glasses, I _____ see the screen.

    a. can't   **b.** won't be able to   **c.** wouldn't

28. You _____ leave the room until the examination is over.

    a. can't   **b.** couldn't   **c.** may not

29. I can't vote because I'm 17, and you _____ be 18 before you can vote in this country.

    a. must   **b.** have to   **c.** ought to

30. That intersection is dangerous. They _____ put up a stop sign.

    a. can   **b.** ought to   **c.** should

Answer Key

Chapter 1 The Simple Present

Exercise 1 (p. 1)

1. line 3: helps
    line 4: doesn't complain
    line 5: remembers
    line 6: is
    line 7: loves
    line 7: love
    line 8: have
    line 9: doesn't talk
    line 10: goes
    line 11: comes
    line 12: watches
    line 12: talks
    line 14: sits
    line 15: don't know
    line 15: isn't
    line 16: doesn't seem
    line 18: don't go
    line 19: don't have
    line 20: need
    line 21: doesn't understand
    line 22: do...have

2. simple present

Exercise 2 (p. 2)

2. enjoy
3. see
4. talks
5. argue
6. don't talk
7. watch
8. fixes
9. eats
10. don't get

Exercise 3 (p. 2)

But she speaks English at work and with some friends. Sometimes her friends correct her pronunciation. She doesn't mind that; she thinks it helps her.

Her listening skills are pretty good. She listens to songs in English. She watches movies in English, too. Her brother watches them with her.

Reading and writing are more difficult for her. She doesn't read English very often, and she almost never writes it. She thinks her writing has a lot of grammar mistakes, but maybe she worries too much.

Exercise 4 (p. 3)

A. 2. Are
3. Do
4. Are
5. Does
6. Is
7. Is
8. Does

B. b. 7   c. 2   d. 5   e. 6   f. 8   g. 1   h. 3

Exercise 5 (p. 4)

2. do most people go to work?
3. people use public transportation to go to work?
4. do most people retire?
5. televisions do most families have?
6. do many people do after high school?
7. do most Americans move?
8. do most American women marry?

Exercise 6 (p. 5)

A. 2. f
3. a
4. b
5. c
6. e

B. b. 1   c. 5   d. 2   e. 4   f. 3

Exercise 7 (p. 6)

The two seasons ~~is~~ *are* summer and winter. Summer ~~go~~ *goes* from April to October. In summer it gets very hot. The temperature sometimes ~~reach~~ *reaches* 40° Celsius. It also ~~rain~~ *rains* a lot in summer. Winter in my country ~~begin~~ *begins* in November. In winter, it is cooler, and it *does* not rain very much. I like the weather better in the winter because I *don't* ~~no~~ like hot weather.

Exercise 8 (p. 6)

Answers will vary.

Chapter 2 Imperatives

Exercise 1 (p. 7)

1. line 4: Go   line 9: Drive
   line 5: Turn   line 10: Turn
   line 7: Stay   line 14: Drive
   line 8: Make   line 15: call

2. Yes, but we don't usually say or write the subject *(you)* when using imperatives.

Exercise 2 (p. 8)

2. Let go of the hand brake.
3. Put the car into drive.
4. Check the rearview mirror.
5. Turn the steering wheel to the right.
6. Don't go so fast.

Exercise 3 (p. 8)

2. have
3. Know
4. don't panic
5. don't go
6. go
7. check
8. don't move
9. don't use

Exercise 4 (p. 9)

2. a
3. h
4. c
5. d
6. b
7. f
8. g

Exercise 5 (p. 9)

2. Check   7. Fasten
3. Arrive   8. drink
4. Bring   9. Chew
5. Remove   10. Enjoy
6. listen

Exercise 6 (p. 10)

2. Let me see, please.   request
3. Don't worry about it.   advice
4. Have a seat.   offer
5. Get up!   command
6. Look out!   warning

Exercise 7 (p. 11)

Answers will vary.

Exercise 8 (p. 11)

Answers will vary.

Chapter 3 The Present Continuous

Exercise 1 (p. 12)

1. line 5: is breaking   line 6: 's blowing
   line 6: 's waiting   line 11: 'm leaving

2. *be* + base form of verb + *ing*

Exercise 2 (p. 13)

2. 'm looking
3. is shining
4. are playing
5. 're wearing
6. 're not thinking/aren't thinking
7. 're having
8. is spraying
9. 're not/aren't running
10. 're trying
11. 's not/isn't letting
12. is telling
13. 's not/isn't paying
14. are laughing
15. 're getting

Exercise 3 (p. 14)

2. How are your friends traveling?
3. Who's the boss talking to?
4. Why is that child crying?
5. Where are Susan and John going?
6. Who's following us?

Exercise 4 (p. 14)

2. It's raining
3. It rains
4. it's raining
5. It rains
6. it's raining
7. It rains
8. It's raining

Exercise 5 (p. 15)

1. b. He's studying in the library at the moment.
   c. My favorite TV show is starting.
2. a. I'm taking three science classes this semester.
   b. For now, I'm staying with Maria.
   c. Luisa and I are trying to get an apartment together.
3. And rents are going up all the time.
4. a. I don't have an apartment right now.
   b. But the apartments seem very expensive.

Exercise 6 (p. 16)

2. 're talking, don't understand
3. 're building, doesn't have
4. doesn't seem, 's working
5. thinks, 's not/isn't studying
6. Do (you) know, 's acting

Exercise 7 (p. 16)

Answers will vary.

See page 75 for Key to Review: Chapters 1–3.

Chapter 4 The Simple Past

Exercise 1 (p. 19)

1. line 2: were   line 7: was
   line 3: was   line 16: was
   line 4: was   line 21: wasn't

2. line 8: tried   line 18: returned
   line 10: believed   line 20: wanted
   line 15: loved   line 22: advised

3. line 12: went   line 15: found
   line 14: took   line 20: told

Exercise 2 (p. 20)

2. were
3. was
4. were
5. was
6. was
7. were
8. were

Exercise 3 (p. 20)

I learned a lot in his class. First, he explained things clearly. When two words had similar meanings, he showed us the difference in a simple way. Time went by quickly in his class. We didn't get bored.

Mr. Kennedy didn't have favorites. He spent time with everyone. He didn't make comments about the weaker students. He encouraged them and helped them a lot. He knew everyone's name by the second class. He was everyone's favorite teacher, and he really enjoyed teaching.

Exercise 4 (p. 21)

2. Were your parents very happy in Colombia?
3. Did your parents come to the U.S. in 1998?
4. Did your father want to move to the U.S.?
5. Were your sisters homesick at first?
6. Did your father find work?

Exercise 5 (p. 21)

2. a. What did Leonardo da Vinci paint?
   b. Who painted the *Mona Lisa*?
3. a. What began in 1848?
   b. When did the California Gold Rush begin?
4. a. Who won the Nobel Peace Prize in 1993?
   b. When did Nelson Mandela win the Nobel Peace Prize?

Exercise 6 (p. 22)

1. b, c
2. d, e
3. a, b
4. c, d, e

Exercise 7 (p. 22)

2. I used to go there every summer.
3. No change
4. I used to love working on the farm.
5. I used to take very good care of the animals.
6. No change

Exercise 8 (p. 23)

I was sad when I left my home country, especially
                                                said
when I ~~say~~ good-bye to my friends.

                                              wasn't
   At the beginning, living in the U.S. ~~isn't~~ easy for me.
                                       was
In those days, the language ~~is~~ hard for me because I
didn't   didn't
~~don't~~ speak it very well. Also, my parents ~~don't~~ speak
                                        helped
English at all then, so I ~~help~~ them. A few months after I
                                              became
came here, I met some people who ~~become~~ my friends.
        made
This ~~makes~~ a big difference in my life at that time. After I
met   felt
~~meet~~ them, I ~~feel~~ more confident.
                                          have
   Now I am going to school, I ~~had~~ some friends, and my

English is better, too.

Exercise 9 (p. 23)

Answers will vary.

Chapter 5 The Past Continuous and Past Time Clauses

Exercise 1 (p. 24)

line 3:   were flashing
line 9:   was crying
line 10: were holding
line 11: was going down

line 13: was raining
line 16: were rushing
line 21: were waiting

Exercise 2 (p. 25)

2. We were eating lunch in the cafeteria
3. You were sitting on the deck
4. The sun was shining
5. The boys were walking to the park

Exercise 3 (p. 25)

2. Who were you studying with?
3. Where were you studying?
4. Why were you studying?
5. Where were you sitting?

Exercise 4 (p. 26)

2. After the rain stopped, we walked home.
3. When Keiko got home, she was exhausted.
4. Hanna moved to Los Angeles after she graduated from college.
5.   While Paulo was on his vacation, he felt relaxed.

Exercise 5 (p. 26)

2. a
3. b
4. b
5. a

Exercise 6 (p. 27)

2. b   7. b
3. b   8. a
4. b   9. b
5. a   10. a
6. a

Exercise 7 (p. 28)

A. 2. T
        3. T
        4. F
        5. F
        6. T
        7. F
        8. T
        9. T
       10. F

B. 4. He made copies after he took notes in the meeting.
        5. He made copies after he took notes in the meeting.
        7. While Bob was making phone calls, the fax machine jammed.
       10. Bob went to lunch after he received a fax.

Exercise 8 (p. 29)

When I ~~was reaching~~ *reached* to the corner of Broadway and Stockton, I stopped because the light was red. I was waiting for the light to change, and suddenly someone ~~was tapping~~ *tapped* me once on the shoulder. Who was it? I turned around to find out. A man ~~were~~ *was* standing behind me. When the light changed, I began to walk really fast. But every time I looked behind me, I ~~was seeing~~ *saw* the man. Finally, I went into a drugstore to escape him. Ten minutes later I ~~was coming~~ *came* out. The man was still outside! He came up to me and spoke. "Are you Susie Lin?" he asked. "I'm your cousin from Vancouver."

Exercise 9 (p. 29)

Answers will vary.

Chapter 6 The Present Perfect

Exercise 1 (p. 30)

1. line 15: have visited
   line 16: have...traveled

   line 19: have been
   line 27: has covered

2. *have/has* + past participle

Exercise 2 (p. 31)

2. ridden
3. eaten
4. met
5. flown
6. found

Answers: Yes, I have/No, I haven't.

Exercise 3 (p. 31)

2. Where have you traveled to?
3. How many people has she invited?
4. Who has been to China?
5. Why have you chosen that book?
6. How long has Larry lived there?
7. What have you prepared for lunch?
8. How much money have you spent this week?

Exercise 4 (p. 32)

2. b
3. a
4. b
5. b
6. a

Exercise 5 (p. 32)

2. since
3. for
4. for
5. since
6. for
7. since
8. since

Exercise 6 (p. 33)

2. 've wanted/have wanted
3. left
4. worked
5. was
6. played
7. gave
8. worked
9. 've had/have had
10. Have you ever had
11. 've looked after/have looked after

Exercise 7 (p. 33)

Answers will vary. Some examples are:
2. We've raised $5,700 so far. / So far we've raised $5,700. / We've already raised $5,700. / We've raised $5,700 already.
3. He's never been to Europe. / He hasn't been to Europe yet. / He still hasn't been to Europe. / He hasn't been to Europe so far. / So far he hasn't been to Europe.
4. They've already interviewed five people. / They've interviewed five people already. / They've interviewed five people so far. / So far they've interviewed five people.

Exercise 8 (p. 34)

We've visited cousins in Australia, and we ~~been~~ to New Zealand twice. We've also ~~went~~ *gone* on safari in Africa. We've been to Europe a lot. Gina and I ~~has~~ *have* spent time in Paris, in Madrid, and in several cities in Italy. We haven't ~~to~~ *been/gone* to Eastern Europe yet, though. We hope to visit Prague and Budapest next year.

My sister Betty was born in the United States, and she has never traveled outside the country—except once when she was very young. But she ~~have~~ *has* been to a lot of places in the U.S. She has ~~visit~~ *visited* most of the national parks: the Grand Canyon, Yellowstone, Yosemite, and so on. She has been to all of the big cities, too. In fact, she ~~is~~ *has* lived in four different cities in the U.S.: New York, Boston, Los Angeles, and San Francisco. I think she *'s* seen more of her own country than most people.

Exercise 9 (p. 34)

Answers will vary.

See page 75 for Key to Review: Chapters 4–6.

Chapter 7 Future Time: *Be Going To, Will, and the Present Continuous*

Exercise 1 (p. 37)

1. line 13: 'm going to clean
   line 15: is going to give
   line 16: 's going to help
2. line 11: won't need   line 13: will be
   line 11: 'll save   line 16: 'll be
   line 12: 'll . . . save   line 17: 'll write
3. line 6: 're moving in

Exercise 2 (p. 38)

2. Are you going to have a big wedding?
3. We're not/We aren't going to have a big celebration.
4. Is it going to rain tomorrow?
5. What are you going to do?
6. I'm going to stay home and read a book.

Exercise 3 (p. 38)

2. When will he find out the results?
3. Where will we/you go?
4. Who will be there?
5. When/What time will the photos be ready?
6. How long will it take?

Exercise 4 (p. 39)

He'll get back at 6:45, take a shower, and shave. He'll go downstairs at 7:00. He'll make a cup of coffee, but he won't drink it. He'll take it with him in his car. He won't eat anything, either. Then he'll drive to work. He'll have breakfast at his desk.

Exercise 5 (p. 39)

A. 2. e
3. f
4. c
5. a
6. b

B. a. 5   b. 2, 6   c. 3, 4

Exercise 6 (p. 40)

1. b. I think we're going to hike up the mountain.
2. a. They say the weather's going to be bad.
   b. You're going to get very wet.
3. a. When are you leaving?
   b. We're leaving here on Wednesday.
   c. Then we're flying home on Sunday.
   d. Where are you going in between?
   e. What are you doing tomorrow?
4. a. Are you and Kate having a good vacation here in Colorado?
   b. We're having a wonderful time.

Exercise 7 (p. 41)

2. S
3. D
4. S
5. S
6. D

Exercise 8 (p. 41)

2. b
3. a
4. a
5. b
6. b

Exercise 9 (p. 42)

Answers will vary.

Chapter 8 Future Time Clauses and *If* Clauses

Exercise 1 (p. 43)

1. line 16: she will be a good student
   line 18: he will travel far
   line 20: she will love food
   line 21: he will become a musician
   The tense used in the main clauses is future with *will*.

2. simple present

Exercise 2 (p. 44)

2. We'll eat / We're going to eat dinner
3. I'll cash / I'm going to cash my paycheck
4. when he turns 68
5. I won't be / I'm not going to be upset
6. we'll celebrate / we're going to celebrate
7. I'll buy / I'm going to buy a new car
8. If you drive too fast

Exercise 3 (p. 44)

2. I'll be ready to leave after I say good-bye to the children.
3. If we don't invite Eric to the party, Sun-Hee will be angry.
4. When Victor gets here, we're going to pick up the car.
5. I'm not going to go swimming if the water's too cold.
6. When the guests arrive, dinner will be ready.

7. If they have another baby, they'll buy a bigger house.
8. I'll look for a job in San Francisco after I graduate.

Exercise 4 (p. 45)

Answers will vary.

Exercise 5 (p. 45)

1. h
2. a, d
3. b, f
4. c, g

Exercise 6 (p. 46)

2. b
3. a
4. b

Exercise 7 (p. 46)

2. If Reiko does well in the interview, she'll get the job. / Reiko will get the job if she does well in the interview.
3. After I lose 10 pounds, I'm going to join a gym. / I'm going to join a gym after I lose 10 pounds.
4. When the movie ends, I'll call you. / I'll call you when the movie ends.
5. If we make too much noise, the baby will wake up. / The baby will wake up if we make too much noise.
6. We're going to eat dinner before we listen to the radio. / Before we listen to the radio, we're going to eat dinner.
7. After Matt buys the groceries, he will go to the bank. / Matt will go to the bank after he buys the groceries.
8. If Ana reads more books, she will increase her vocabulary. / Ana will increase her vocabulary if she reads more books.

Exercise 8 (p. 47)

Answers will vary.

See page 75 for Key to Review: Chapters 7–8.

Chapter 9 Modals of Ability and Possibility

Exercise 1 (p. 50)

1. line 4: can   line 8: Can
   line 4: will   line 8: might not
   line 6: will   line 9: can
   line 6: may   line 9: could
   line 7: won't

2. ✓ Each modal has only one form.
                    don't
   ____ Modals ⋀ agree with the subject.

Exercise 2 (p. 51)

A. 2. I can't ski.
   3. Can you drive?
   4. They can play several instruments.

B. 1. We couldn't see anything.
2. Could you play the piano when you were younger?
3. They couldn't tell me anything.
4. Could Tomek understand that?

Exercise 3 (p. 51)

A. 2. When could he get here?
3. How long could it take?
4. What could go wrong?

B. 1. What kind of car will you get?
2. How will you pay the bills?
3. What time will he get there?
4. Who will be there?

Exercise 4 (p. 52)

2. can't, will be able to
3. can, will be able to
4. won't be able to
5. won't be able to, will be able to
6. will be able to

Exercise 5 (p. 53)

2. Correct
3. Incorrect, was able to
4. Correct
5. Incorrect, were able to

Exercise 6 (p. 53)

Exercise 7 (p. 54)

2. b
3. b
4. c
5. a
6. b

Exercise 8 (p. 54)

Answers will vary.

Chapter 10 Modals and Phrases of Request, Permission, Desire, and Preference

Exercise 1 (p. 55)

2. C, Could
3. B, Can
4. A, would
5. C, Would
6. A, 'd
7. B, Can
8. A, 'd
9. B, Could
10. C, 'd

Exercise 2 (p. 56)

2. May I have some more coffee?
3. Would you take my picture?
4. When could I see you tomorrow?
5. Can I have something to eat?
6. Will you give me a ride?

Exercise 3 (p. 56)

2. I'd prefer not to take a class on Fridays.
3. What time would Takeshi like to leave?
4. My mother would rather not come with us.
5. Would you prefer milk or juice?
6. I'd like to live in a big city.

Exercise 4 (p. 57)

2. a. Can I talk to you after class?
   b. May I please talk to you after class?
3. a. Can you say that again?
   b. Would you say that again, please?
4. a. Would you drop me off at the corner, please?
   b. Can you drop me off at the corner?

Exercise 5 (p. 57)

2. 'd prefer
3. 'd rather
4. 'd rather
5. Would...like
6. 'd like
7. Would...prefer/Would...like
8. 'd like

Exercise 6 (p. 58)

2. b
3. a
4. a
5. c
6. b
7. b
8. c
9. b
10. a

Exercise 7 (p. 59)

Answers will vary.

Chapter 11 Modals and Phrasal Modals of Advice, Necessity, and Prohibition

Exercise 1 (p. 60)

1. line 6:   could
   line 11: must
   line 12: should
   line 15: 'd better
   line 19: should
   line 24: ought to
   line 29: have to
   line 33: should

2. line 6:   collect
   line 11: consider
   line 12: try
   line 15: choose
   line 19: learn
   line 24: know
   line 29: know
   line 33: be

Exercise 2 (p. 61)

2. to go
3. to go
4. go
5. go
6. go
7. to go
8. to go
9. go
10. to go

Exercise 3 (p. 61)

2. Who should she tell?
3. When do they have to leave?
4. How long do you have to stay?
5. When does he have to tell her?
6. What should Emily do?
7. Who should I ask?
8. How often should we exercise?

Exercise 4 (p. 62)

2. b
3. b
4. a
5. b
6. b

Exercise 5 (p. 62)

Chris: You ~~could~~ *must/have (got) to* show your passport and your visa.

Satomi: OK. And how do I get to the university?

Chris: Well, you ~~have to~~ *could/might* take public transportation, but it's probably better to take a taxi.

Satomi: How much will that cost?

Chris: About $30. But you ~~might~~ *should/ought* add a tip for the taxi driver. That's my advice—almost everyone tips. We usually tip about 15 percent.

Satomi: I see. What about money? What's the best way to keep my money?

Chris: Well, you could use traveler's checks, or you ~~must~~ *could/might* open a bank account.

Exercise 6 (p. 63)

2. must
3. must not
4. must
5. must
6. don't have to
7. must
8. must
9. don't have to

Exercise 7 (p. 63)

2. a
3. b
4. b
5. a
6. a

Exercise 8 (p. 64)

Answers will vary.

See page 76 for Key to Review: Chapters 9–11.

Key to Chapter Reviews

Review: Chapters 1–3 (p. 17)

A.
1. What fish go to heaven?
2. What flowers do you have on your face?
3. When does an old clock die?
4. What words have the most letters?
5. Why does a giraffe have a long neck?
6. When does a doctor get angry?

B.
7. Today is Saturday, and Alex is ~~stay~~ *staying* at home with his family.
8. His mother ~~makes~~ *is making* a chocolate cake in the kitchen.
9. The cake ~~is smelling~~ *smells* great.
10. His father is outside. He ~~washes~~ *'s washing* his car.
11. His sister, Tina, is ~~listen~~ *listening* to music in her bedroom.
12. She is playing it too loud, and Alex ~~is hearing~~ *hears* it in the basement.
13. His sister, Sara, is ~~plays~~ *playing* a video game in the living room.
14. Everybody ~~is seeming~~ *seems* very happy.

C.
15. a
16. b
17. c
18. c
19. a
20. c
21. b
22. b
23. b
24. a
25. c
26. a
27. c
28. a
29. a
30. b

Review: Chapters 4–6 (p. 35)

A.
1. said
2. threw
3. heard
4. flew
5. bought
6. begun
7. sold
8. eaten
9. worn
10. gave
11. fell
12. grown
13. bit
14. lost

B.
15. Not OK
16. OK
17. Not OK
18. OK
19. Not OK
20. Not OK
21. OK

C.
22. c
23. c
24. a
25. c
26. b
27. a
28. c
29. b
30. b

Review: Chapters 7–8 (p. 48)

A.
1. I~~ll~~ *'m* meeting John after work. / I'll meet John after work.
2. We *'re* not going to Los Angeles this summer.
3. I have an idea: I'~~m~~ *ll* pick you up on my way to the airport.
4. Can you turn off the light when you ~~are leaving~~ *leave* the room?
5. Will you ~~being~~ *be* at the party tomorrow?
6. When she ~~will arrive~~ *arrives* home, she will phone her mother.
7. I *'m* going to tell you.
8. This test isn't ~~being~~ easy.

B.
9. b
10. b
11. a
12. a
13. a
14. b
15. a
16. b

C.
17. a
18. c
19. c
20. b
21. a
22. c
23. b
24. b
25. a
26. a
27. b

28. c
29. a
30. c

Review: Chapters 9–11 (p. 65)

A.
1. b
2. a
3. a
4. b
5. a
6. b

B.
7. It might not rain.
8. I wouldn't like to be in his situation.
9. He doesn't have to do it.
10. We'd better not go now.
11. They'd prefer not to wait.
12. She shouldn't leave.
13. He may not come.

C.
14. It's really late. We really should ~~to~~ go home.

15. You don't have ~~got~~ to worry about dinner. Rosa has agreed to cook.

16. Yesterday I ~~could~~ *was able to* run a mile in less than six minutes.

17. They would (not) rather work late tonight.

18. Where would you like *to* go to college?

19. It's a long way to the station. I'd prefer to drive rather *than* walk.

20. Susan might help~~s~~ with our math homework.

21. When we lived in Africa, we ~~could~~ *were able to/could* see elephants and giraffes.

D.
22. a, b
23. b, c
24. a, c
25. b, c
26. a, c
27. a, b
28. a, c
29. a, b
30. b, c